The Black Dawg

An illustrated poem about Depression and Hope

by Louis McIntosh & Kathryn Hockey

The process of writing and illustrating The Black Dawg poem has helped us both to recognise, understand and explain what we go through when we are depressed.

We hope that fellow sufferers will recognise their symptoms and realise that they are not alone. We also hope that reading The Black Dawg may help friends and family to better understand the dark journey that their loved ones take unwillingly.

"I am motivated by a passionate need to articulate depression and diffuse the stigma around it."
Louis McIntosh 2016

Published by Black Dawg Publishing 2016
www.kathrynhockey.com/the-black-dawg/

ISBN: 978-0-9954617-0-3

Printed in the UK by Charlesworth Press

SOS, in distress, I've lost me again
Drowning in that deep, dark sea again
Serve my penance till I'm free again
Someday...someday soon

Disengage from life's mad pace
Put on fake brave smiley face
Dislocate from love's embrace
When I need it most

Munch's Scream inside my head
Pollock's splatters, my mind's thread
Dali's dripping world my dread
...Today

Leave stubble there
Don't comb my hair
Each day the same dull clothes I wear
Look in the fridge, the cupboard's bare
Can't face a meal, don't care, don't care

Black Dawg chatter fills my mind
With twisted logic so unkind
Telling me what's wrong is right
And right is wrong
Too weak to fight

The lies my brain doth feed to me
Down darkened paths it leadeth me
Convincing what will be will be
Five fathoms deep in murky sea

With mental chains of slavery
A paranoid conspiracy
When fiction's fact I let it be
Helplessly

Pleasure principle put to the sword
A sandwich tastes like old cardboard
Should I take a trip to Lourdes?
Bathe Me, Bless Me...Could I be Cured?

Every day becomes the same to Me
Sunday, Monday, Blackday, Blackday
Will I wake to another Crap day?
Wishing one day, spring the trap day?

I can't think, my brain's in clink
Synapses creak, they creak, they creak
Can't form the words to even speak
Will it last an hour, a week?
Lifts as a cloud but returns at peak
Leaving me weak, so weak, so weak

I try to hide but it can see Me
I try to fight with all my might
I try to seek the Fears that Bleed me
Black Dawg stalks me day and night

When I wake the dawn is breaking
But my soul is bathed in night
I cannot think, my brain is aching
While my soul is searching light

Please God when the Black Dawg calls
And creates these prison walls
Help me overcome the falls
And rise again

It's cold and lonely in this place
I want to join the human race
I need some hope and time and space
To rise again

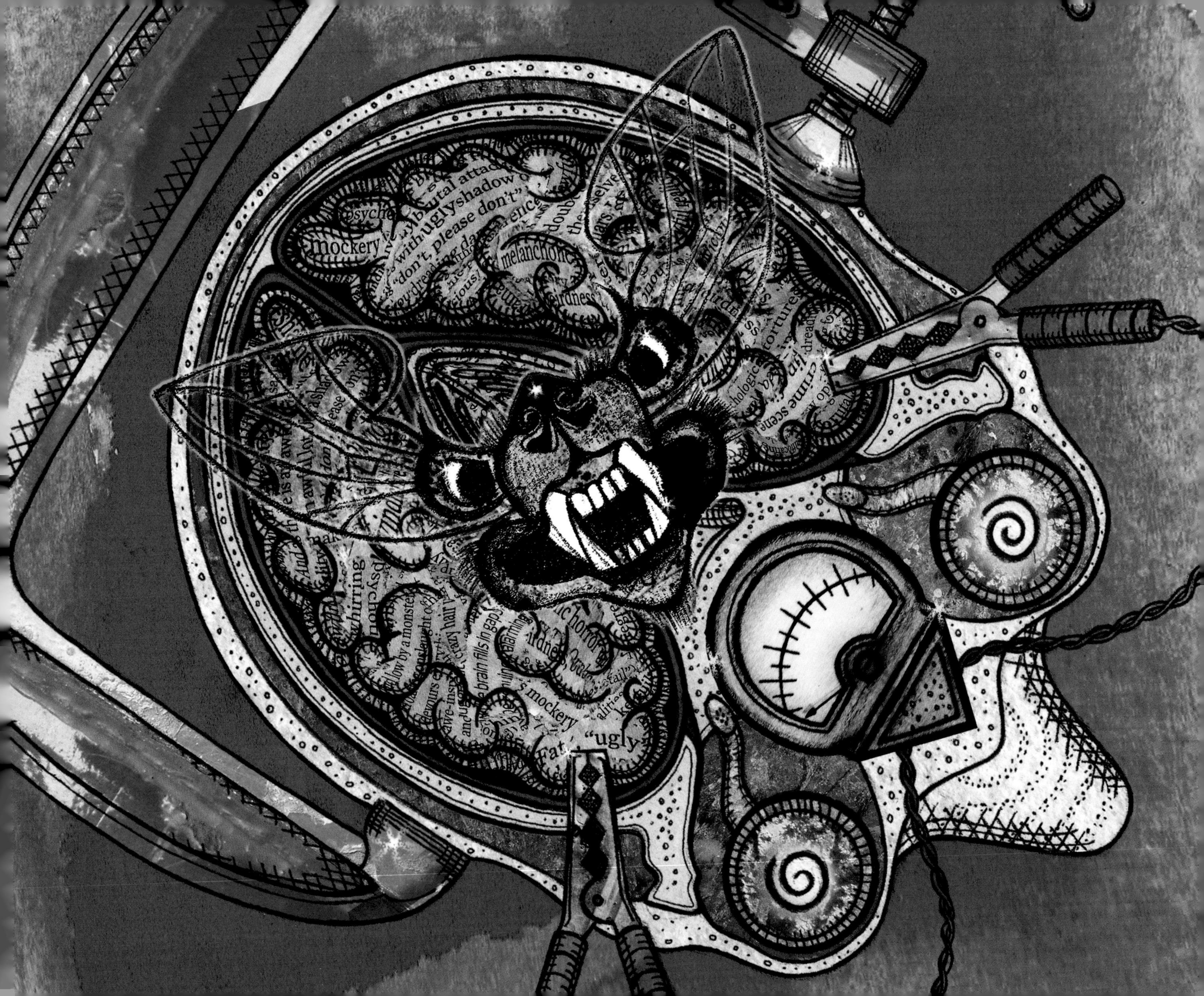
mockery
"don't, please don't"
weirdness
crime scene
brain fills in gaps
mockery
"ugly"

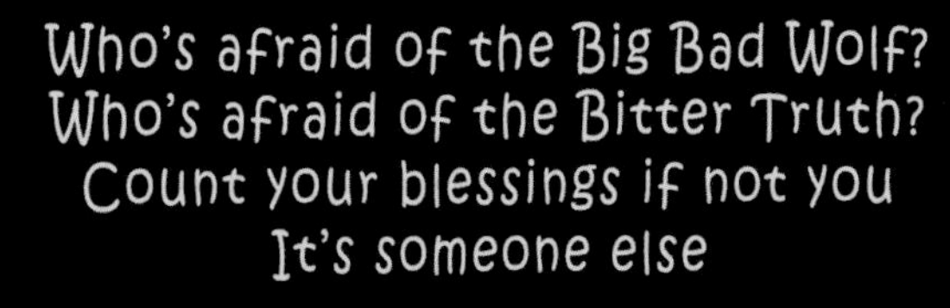

Who's afraid of the Big Bad Wolf?
Who's afraid of the Bitter Truth?
Count your blessings if not you
It's someone else

Rich, young, old or poor
You can find him at your door
You want less but he wants more
You need a friend

You need a friend, you need a friend
One on whom you can depend
To be around
When your ship's aground
When your chips are down
When your smile's a frown

These are not laughter lines, I'm frowning
With a will that's slowly drowning
My eyes set to dull,
Sunk in sockets in my skull
Behind them my brain is full
With mush and thoughts I cannot cull

Don't pity me or offer sage advice
I cannot hear though you may tell me twice
How are you? As you try to be so nice
And Black Dawg tightens up the vice

All the rainbow colours turn to black
Black is black, I want Me back
As I crawl into the sack
In mourning for the spark I lack

It's here, there and everywhere
The dread that lurks behind mad stare
And I don't care what clothes I wear
And I don't wash or comb my hair
And still the fridge and cupboard's bare
Can't eat a meal, don't care, don't care!

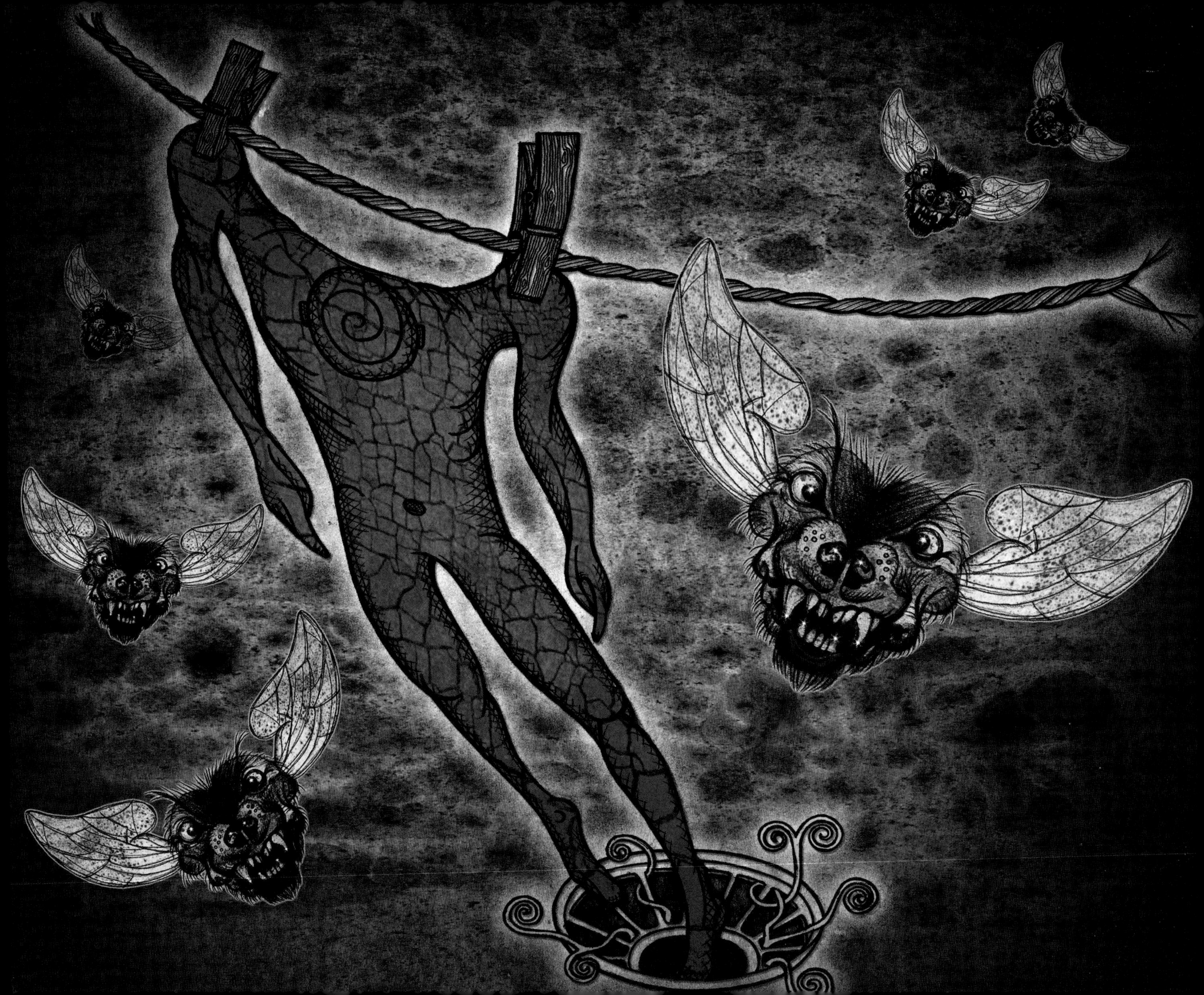

He lurks in shadows, abhors the Light
Abhors Beauty, abhors Love
Pours scorn on me from above
Tells me lies
Breaks friendship ties
A thief of souls with no holds barred
Leaving me wounded, scared and scarred

Bring me back to Normal fast
God please help, don't make it last
Answer my prayers, Unlock the Past
To find some Reason's all I ask
To help me tread the truthful path
Not stumbling blindly, Hurt and Lost

Give me back the Life I had
Before this Black Dawg sent me Mad
With Impotence, Fear and Loathing Life
When Dawg descends it is no Hype
Believe me then I'd swap my Head
With refugee with no sure bed
To ward away this Endless Dread

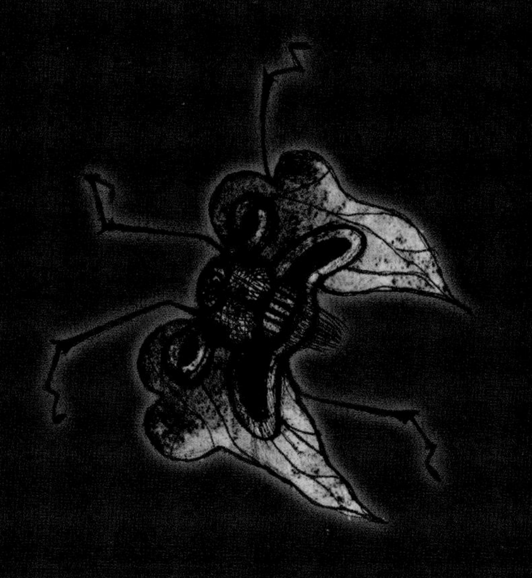

So when Dawg calls and You climb the Walls
Like trying to swim Niagara Falls
You Slump or Crouch and can't stand Tall
Here's what to do, a Battle Call

Bundle Black Dawg into Sack
Tie with rope and Club him, Thwack!
Best defense should be Attack
So AttackAttackAttackAttackAttack

Spiral Down into Depression
Now Spiral Up and learn a Lesson
How to Fight Back
How to Cope
How to Manage
How to Hope
How to smile without a reason
Do you need one? Answer: Nope

Spiralling branches, silent sky
Feel composed and rested, whole
Dark Clouds dissipate, goodbye
Now heal my hung, drawn, quartered Soul

Enjoy your brief spell on this earth
Love, live, breathe and know your worth
To keep in check Dawg's stubborn Curse
As you mend a Mind that's braved the worst

They say each Dog will have its Day
Well listen Black Dawg, No! No way!
The Time has come to keep you at Bay
And Rise Again

Sound of Laughter long forgotten
Feeling Good, then Great, a sudden
Surge of hormones Floods My Body
Toxic Waste now leaves My Body
Brain engage and Rule My Body
Cos all I wish is that My Body
Works the same as Everbody's

Is that really much to Ask?
Is my Mind up to the task?
Fight Depression; finish last
Or banish it to Murky Past
Say Free at Last, Free at Last
Bye bye Blues, new Die is Cast

Sooooo, Here we Go

Weed the garden

Ping some Pong

Spur of Mo, Break into Song

It's for your Soul, it can't be Wrong

Bang a Drum

Expel Frustration

You might discover mild Elation

Hold a Baby

Stroke a Cat

Hug a friend, we all like that!

Wear bright clothes and Funky Hat

If you need, take Happy Pills

But be cautious of cheap thrills

Look into your Heart and Soul

Roll the Dice

Be whole, Be Whole

Huge thanks to those who made it possible to publish **The Black Dawg**

Jane Alicia Cooney David Milward Terry West Mark Ford Bob Cunningham
Drew Harrison Rich Hadley Ron & Mary Hockey Sasha Stuart Penny Ladds
Sylvia Elsi Currie Robert Dare Joe Brooking Les Go Sharon Tafft Lisa
Barry Karobik Patrick Bennett Louise Palmer-Masterton Geraldine Lambe
Laurence Bower Viet Bui Xuan Mark Bennett Philippe Young Nan Tricker
Sarah Houlding Jules & Jess Whitacker Emma Weatherstone Karen Ormiston

Judith Morgan Kelly Lawler Jackie Cornwall Javier Melian Sallie Walker Susan Power
Angela Katy Sender Rachel Chalaye Christopher Dunn Ellie Cormie Steve Gaz Coleman
Ian & Uta Corinna Barrell George Pilgrim Joyce Wycoff Rick Patton Andi Notloh Sophie
Johnny Edwardes James Barrett Gareth Walker Gill Williams Josie Louis McIntosh
Michael Howard Christian Kämpfe Anne Middlekamp Sarah Gibson Debra Berger Rhian
Vanessa Bonnin Debby Ray Lois Cousins Bryony Persson Wanda Miller Alastair Chisholm
Penny Smith Aline Davis Nicholas Allan Lynne Parish Tony Briggs Juan Pedro Álvarez
Tara Andrew Zionts Claire Tyler Craig Tyler Chris Meacock Anne Manson Keith Lomas
Dipak Michi Mathias Barbara Schuler Liz Harvey Tammy Andrew Cooke Els Lehr
Sara Dale Rodriguez Chardonnay Bell Claudia Kaiser Mike Brassey Tejumade Alakija
Roy & Sue Stubbings Joanna Crowson Chris Indi Davidson Alex Findlow James Stuart
Sue Anne & Sean Rawnsley Miriam Reik Antiguo Correo Marc Ralph Deborah Wakins
Nadine Pilar Cadenas Montañés Tino Rawnsley Shaun Clarke Amit Kvint Limor Kamin
Emma Ashman-Clark Tina Westwood Michelle Hayslip Westley Gibbons Scott Shillum
Colette Niall Deegan Gerd Bellinger Vincent Bottomley Maurice O'Connor Kat Griff
Richard Nacht Sabine Friedrich Morgan Caney Sarah Steeples Helen Wheat Lourdes